Laurie Duggan | Homer Street

New Poems

GIRAMONDO POETS

Laurie Duggan | Homer Street

First published 2020
from the Writing and Society Research Centre
at Western Sydney University
by the Giramondo Publishing Company
PO Box 752
Artarmon NSW 1570 Australia
www.giramondopublishing.com

Cover image: Rachel Ellis
Late Afternoon, lower Keppel Street, Bathurst, 2007
58 x 44 cm, oil on board

Cover design by Jenny Grigg
Layout designed by Harry Williamson
Typeset by Andrew Davies
in 10/16.5 pt Baskerville BT

Printed and bound by Ligare Book Printers
Distributed in Australia by NewSouth Books

A catalogue record for this
book is available from the
National Library of Australia.

ISBN: 978-1-925818-46-8

Acknowledgements

Six of the 'Afterimages' poems appeared in *No Particular Place To Go* (Shearsman, 2017). Two more poems from this series are revisions of pieces published earlier: 'Dorothy Napangardi' appeared as 'Positive Black' in *The Passenger* (UQP, 2006) while 'David Stachan' appeared as 'Homage to the Charm School' in *Mangroves* (UQP, 2003). Nicholas Pounder's Polar Bear Press published a limited edition of some of the 'Afterimages' in 2018. Other poems have appeared in various magazines on and offline: *Australian Poetry Journal*, *Broadsheet* (NZ), *Coolabah*, *Golden Handcuffs Review* (USA), *Intercapilliary Space* (UK), *Molly Bloom* (UK), *Otoliths*, *Overland*, *Rabbit*, *Read On*, *Marrickville Pause* and *Tears in the Fence* (UK). My thanks to all the editors.

Previous collections by Laurie Duggan

The Ash Range

The Epigrams of Martial

Blue Notes

Adventures In Paradise

Memorials

New and Selected Poems 1971–1993

Mangroves

The Passenger

The Collected Blue Hills

East & Under the Weather

Selected Poems 1971–2017

Contents

A Preface

songs of myself
the Americans sing

no sense
of insignificance

'you're not there'
said Basil
Brooklyn 1992

he was right

1

A Closing Album

Dublin

the lane outside
dead quiet at 9 am

after a night of
'Suspicious minds'

later: the rattle of kegs,
a truckload of empties

in the supermarket
a Product Recall for Durex condoms

on the street 'Love will tear us apart'
sung with a lilt

East Kent

fresh hops above the bar
mist on the London train

it's the poetry season

Faversham

dead lupin stalks cut down
the sun angles through back windows

Bridport

a wall of sand
between the car park and the English Channel

Blandford Forum

the sky alternates
dark and light

over these Georgians
this one-way traffic

memory: a blue yacht
in an attic window

Gillingham

Rotund, pink
and pissed

the English sing
their football songs

Southbank

A glass lift reveals the movement of habitués
up and down the nearest building
its façade bolted together with tensile struts,

an airliner climbs from London City across a gap
where evening light falls between apartments and offices,

below this, a dignitary on a plinth
faces the distant rail bridge

None of this had to happen.

Lambeth

the arms of chairs become swans
and the lamp posts are coiled fish
a mad voice chants for no-one in particular

a sign reads: KEEP CALM – HAVE A COFFEE
"Friday – Saturday . . . for shark's fins . . ."
(a cyclist outside the Archbishop's palace)

William Blake stares across the Thames
at the shrouded Houses of Parliament

Around Sandwich

chalk and marsh
the port well inland

a Viking longboat
just down from the car park

and in the hinterland, a road
that separates Nash from Ash

St Ives

it's a cubist village:
rooftops come apart
and reassemble, edged with lichen,
a pale blue ocean
at the edge of a country

Allotments

Allotment 101

a window
re-hung
on Leigh Street

sunlight and heat
up on the rooftops

shade, a slight
movement of air

Allotment 102

pillow

stone

Allotment 103

into the sun
across mudfields

a letterbox
mimics a barn

red berries glow
in a dark landscape

Allotment 104

stillness
a pond

the sun
at angle

outline of
a stile

dark against
dry grass,

then white

an egret
on the marsh

Allotment 105

long shadows
on a ploughed field

distant rumble
of the motorway

Allotment 106

the body
wrapped in down

refuses to
get up

on the street
wet bricks

resist the effort
to walk unless
you lean forward

Allotment 107

in The Yard
the full Kentish

'the coffee's hot
and the toast is brown'

deep soul on the system,
the air outside

heavy with malt –
flurries expected

Allotment 108

the door of the Bloomsbury Room
swings shut,

St George flags ruffled by
cold air off Museum Street;

a man with a basset hound
collects coffee from Ruskin's Café

Allotment 109

barking dogs
turn out to be geese, a flock

over marshland,
mud islands guarded

by a spit
at Church Norton

Allotment 110

A track marked
by broken branches

traverses Redhill Wood
to the pheasant farm; an access road

leads to the dismantled
Southern Line at Bishopsbourne,

home of the orchidist
and the church whose organist

slipped gently off his organ stool.
The Nail Bourne's waterless this year,

up from its bank, cubes
and cylinders cut from a fallen tree

leave a rough negative

Allotment 111

A memory just flashed:

. . . Oxford . . .
                                        . . . a pen knife . . .

. . . amaretto and coffee . . .

Sod the coffee

Allotment 112

orange sky (Sahara dust)

glare of a wet street

Allotment 113

I'm in the yard at Iklectik, too early for the reading. I'm seated on an old lounge chair under a shelter hemmed with hay bales and autumn leaves, a warped geodesic dome to my right. It's a strange oasis on prime developmental land (between Lambeth Palace and Waterloo Station). The last time I was here I heard a nightingale. Now it's distant football practice and the rumble of trains over the viaducts. Will anybody show up? Someone in an adjacent office knocks off, bolts the shutters and turns out the lights. Paper lanterns wave in the breeze. A mangy fox trots down the path. Lights go on in the hall. Someone has entered through a back door. The fox reappears. And a man with an electric keyboard.

Allotment 114

topknot of the Buddha's head
emerges from snow

gaps in the white coverage
for hellebores and daffodils

Allotment 115

snow along hill shadow
and fence line

that edge out of Macclesfield
I walked up in 1992

round the back of Manchester Piccadilly
the façade of a gutted Victorian building

in neon: EVERYTHING IS CONNECTED

Allotment 116

for realism
the right of way
                    from Brogdale Road
blocked by developers

Allotment 117

marsh marigolds
          (kingcups)
at the source of Faversham Creek

Allotment 118

a red kite rides thermals
over Didcot

distant beeches
crown Wittenham clumps

Allotment 119

a decadent walks his butterflies
past Goodnestone chapel to Graveney

too early in the season for the odour
of strawberries

instead, the Creek,
its sewage outfall,

Harveys in the Phoenix
then home

Allotment 120

rain holds off,
holds on.
you too, old son

Allotment 121

flint bands in the chalk
of East Kent

clefts in the rock but
no oracle

no mermaids sing here
each to each

the horizon's clipped
by the square stern of a container

and a sign far end of the beach
reads: SILENCE

Allotment 122

dove coos
rise an octave

dead-headed iris
dyes fingers purple

the household poisons
in blossom:

foxglove
lily-of-the-valley

monkshood

Allotment 123

He lost his head . . .
four pints, a few shots of Sambuca . . .
his kids running around in the garden . . .
talked about Kurt Vonnegut,
things like that . . .
a clever bloke

Allotment 124

windflowers wilt
in the heat

weeds thrive

Allotment 125

a challenge to perspective:
three tall men behind the bar

in the adjoining room
distressed white on brick:

FAVERSHAM

Dogs

Barcode 2

change from a pint
on a silver plate?
time to move on

Transcription Haiku

Japanese compilers
suspect musical pun
On Green Dolphy Street

The Body Politic

get off the fence
step up to the plate
& kick the hot potato
into the long grass

A further misreading

Philip Larkin
the librarian from Hell

Australian Pastoral

a bush muse
amuse bouche

Roadside Memorials

even the dead are
victims of fashion

the once loved defined
by what they once liked

The misanthrope

He liked people who liked people
but he didn't like people

Mysteries of 2018

an overgrown trampoline
in a churchyard

Macon chardonnay
bought for the memory

Philip Whalen's On Bear's Head
nearly 42 years since purchase
red and purple cloth cover
binding starting to come apart

North Carlton

a man steps from a car
with a half bottle of Smirnoff

Mr Blur

the pattern on a lace curtain
resolves into the face of a donkey
then it's Mr Blur

Boxing Day

A deflated Santa
in a parking lot

American Memoir

a head barely appearing above a lecturn
(Hettie Jones, New York, 2014)

The Louis Armstrong Reader

Old Pops's Book of Practical Scats

Autumn

the feel of shoes
strange on
estranged feet

cumulo-cirrus over the office blocks
Japanese tourists in the herb garden

The Ed Dorn Outtake

sitting down
and eating breakfast
oughtn't to be
too much of an ordeal

Domestic collectives

a surfeit of bathmats
a dearth of hand towels

Homage to Guy Debord

under the chips
fake newspaper

2

Six notes for John Forbes

1

At Rae's memorial plaque
unveiled in a square, Summer Hill
I wondered what could be named for you?
A swimming pool perhaps,
where you exorcised asthma?
A car wash on Taylor Street?

2

I wrote to you a few years back
that England wasn't the place you knew
now it's even less so, or more:
the superstructure of class
showing through the fake edifice of 'merit',
all that bedrock pomposity
and servility that characterises the place
as Jacob Rees-Mogg, a seeming parody
turns out to be the real thing.

It was in England that I came to understand
the meaning of 'hegemony'
(where supposed alternatives echo each other,
the newspapers all liking the same poets
those poets published by the same house
– was this 'house style'?

The Houses of Parliament,
the City, made up similarly
of Old Etonians.

Houses, actual houses,
pokier than any on the continent
with a sense of 'little Britain' 'going it alone',
Dunkirk references afloat on the tide
of neoconservatism.

3

Dumped in the skip of history
by the great removalist
you would not have written pages of drivel
to get at a few things. Yours was
a different aesthetic, ethic even;
the poem came as a whole
or it didn't; and then
you revised it.

4

You were Zeus in Ken Searle's painting,
alarmed at the bulk of your torso;
For love you bought
contact lenses, then lost them.

You read Manning Clark, bemused
that God had played such a big part
in Australian history.

5

You walked with us once
on the northern tablelands.
Miles from the nearest bookshop
(or any other sign of life)
you read the fine print on prescription vials.

Elsewhere in that hinterland
from his throne (a collapsed sofa)
'the greatest poet since Yeats'
dismissed you (after your death) as
a 'minor poet' with amusing moments.

6

So far the Harbour's free of landfill.
Brett Whiteley and Ken Done remind us
of our tourist selves,
while down on Woolloomooloo Bay
the navy moors, in view of the Art Gallery,
as though this were some kind of reassurance.

Blue Hills 76

sun on the underside of clouds
a perception of red lakes

then heat

                    a hint of breeze
then stillness

shades of leaves on a kitchen bench

insect furrows in eucalypt bark

Blue Hills 77

the glint of a car through a screen door
a clang of metal gates

at night the clatter of freight trucks
on the Bankstown line

the birds in this vicinity
are large or predatory

no spuggies hereabouts
to fledge

Blue Hills 78

stones in the bottom of a jar
the water yellows

                                        hyssop

    (a crossword clue)

                                    church bells

    (no certain location)

a man carries a cat box across a courtyard

Blue Hills 79

the ridges of this place
thought a flat city
where bins clatter in a bluestone alley,

                                        that basalt edge
runs through Melbourne's west.

someone looks out from a balcony
the way the old pass the time
                                          (texting intently)

noises off:
                            trains the far side of Royal Park
a fire alarm
mimicked by a bird

Blue Hills 80

one of those eucalypts,
pink, vague shape

of a human body,
across the road

from a Boer War veteran
stranded on the median

Blue Hills 81

a change to hit this afternoon
maybe thunder

and then we go
Tropical Skiing

or drinking
on Nicholson Street

the steady roll of dark clouds
south of here

a baroque backdrop
to the city

Blue Hills 82

the balance of colour, shape
and texture
                a painting
of vases, bouquets,
stray objects
                    a shoe, a leaf, a bottle,
a carved bird,
                even a painting
within the painting,
                      perhaps a picket fence

beyond this, the idea that art
might be useful
it might help you to sell something

Blue Hills 83

bluestone groynes,
ti-trees parallel to the ground
shaped by wind from Port Phillip

spiked grasses suck moisture from sand,

the You Yangs, distant southwest,
then the Brisbane Ranges,
container terminals,
the bend of Westgate,

further, the shelf of Macedon

Blue Hills 84

this garden, like the house
resists its environment

the uninviting neatness
of pond and low hedges

nothing to step out into
save these signifiers

concrete imitates stone

imported figurines
guard the mantlepiece

Blue Hills 85

the bend of this river
once paradise
a mingling of salt and fresh
and whatever lived on the ground

what was the name of this place?
(what is the name)
                    and whom to ask?

the rock ledges painted by recent visitors
over a century back

a discovery of light

                    of how to work with underpainting
and not neutralise
the effect of atmosphere

Blue Hills 86

a rectangle of sky
lights the kitchen bench

shadows of screeching corellas
cross this space

a cat perched on the coffee machine, stares
towards the front door, another,
eyes closed, faces north

hieratic

they are the gods of this household

the cat makes the man

Blue Hills 87

art deco façades of Campsie
beneath a bruised sky
all shades of red, blue, grey

evening light, peeling green paint
and Chinese neon

Blue Hills 88

Newtown, 1970s – remember Maurice's Felafel
his quiet dealings with young drunks

Mark Ray's streets of that suburb
before the deluge

flyers from a nether world

I salute their luminous hum

Blue Hills 89

a thunderstorm crosses the city,
an edge of grey cloud
the lighter anvil behind

sheoak, paperbark and mangrove
frame the river

the pattern:
                                        grey, humid morning
cloud-lift
and heat-rise

then a cool breeze from the east

Blue Hills 90

(remember 1971
'night frogs in the dam'?
a frog here, in the pond
awake as I am comatose

different varieties of bark
loose or surface,
the way a tree-fern
constructs itself
almost planned obsolescence

close-by, a bird call, too low-pitched
for a magpie, too complex
for a currawong

'for God's sake shut up'

'shut up is a VERY RUDE WORD'

Blue Hills 91

26 degrees at 8.00 am
uphill, a brace of parrots

leaves hang in total stillness

chance of a storm

I hang around the house

'nobody rings back'

altered shapes of cloud metamorphosis

(no storm)

Blue Hills 92

a fin
cut from metal
a space
with facing tools
spanner and
screwdriver

a figure in stone
behind a broken fence
its base buried in flowering grass

Blue Hills 93

go to Bondi
to sign a colophon

a sea breeze up Birrell St

Blue Hills 94

(as one tree stops
cicada sound shifts to another
intensifies
shifts again

then the first tree resumes

you never see them

Blue Hills 95

the Saturday paper's
heavier thud,

then voices off,
on different schedules

                    if we only knew
what they were

airliners head northwest
over Marrickville

a block away
a cockatoo cracks a seed pod
its eye a black dot

all around
            inscribed tree trunks

the daily scrawl

Blue Hills 96

freight rattles on the Bankstown line
the Eagles die
on a distant car radio

*

I am a tawny frogmouth
a strange bird
perched on a verandah

*

the long claws of waterhens
hold grass blades
for the beak to strip

*

before the clothes repair shop,
a dummy, slightly less than life-size,
calls perspective into question

*

a cat on a sunlit driveway
flicks its tail
and disappears

Blue Hills 97

at Sydenham: a lopsided sub-station
the burnt-out General Gordon hotel

the shadow of an airliner
bigger than the plane itself

Blue Hills 98

what to leave out
(the detail of all those tiles
instead of the sweep
of a roof
                                    the art
of knowing when to stop

Blue Hills 99

fawn
& pink,
grey
& brown,
stringy
or smooth,
shaded
or inscribed

(eucalypt surfaces)

*

angophora, that
red-pink wood
all over Ball's Head,
easy to find, unlike
apostrophes on maps;
a ferry leaving McMahon's Point
named (appropriately): MAY GIBBS

Blue Hills 100

enter this landscape through sandstone
                    scored by pickmarks
a tunnel with absolutely vertical sides
skylit at intervals

observe the displacement of species
(angophora), the shift of habitat
down the hills to Berry's Bay

note the archaeology of these coves
amphitheatres that were once oil tanks,

        the owners still here, bemused
        at the antics of visitors

on Ball's Head
an elder sits at a picnic table

a brush turkey treads ashes
under a rock shelf

Blue Hills 101

the dresser, its photographs
                    an archaeology of family,
eyes of a wooden god
                    downcast, as though ironing;
on the base of a lamp
                    a sulphur-crested cockatoo
perches on a gum sprig,
                    the shade's cone above it
fawn cloth over white china

Blue Hills 102

slight movement of banksia,
a burst of thunder, but no rain

an hour later the change hits,
a mass of cloud northwest

surface tension at the edge
                    as water settles
on oiled wood
                              aircraft lift
through the turbulence

Blue Hills 103

wit wit wit
said the bird
  a noisy miner
  not a nosy parker

later still – is it a man primalling
or an engine revved?
  (above it, a kookaburra
  from the canopy,
  a currawong on the nearby roof,
  then nervous parrot flight

it's true, there are no sparrows here
the birds know something we don't

Blue Hills 104

upstream from Tallangatta
oxbows, salt-pans and marshes
once the Murray drops from its source,
the Indi, near Corryong

I travelled down there
thirty years ago, on backroads
in a rented car
                    spent two days
at the pub in Jingellic
                              is it still there?

Blue Hills 105

there's a point when aerial photographs
join awkwardly as though
some place escapes the net

it could be nowhere
unless on the ground
looking up at a blank piece of sky

Blue Hills 106

next door, someone vacuums a car
it's what the new year comes to

fern shadow on smooth trunk
a ribcage
                    (and where
in all this merriment
is the tawny frogmouth?

a phone simulates a phone
                                        the shout
          'get out now!' possibly
                    directed at a child

just as you decide to close windows
a zephyr starts
from the Cooks River

inside:
Paul Kelly's 'Gossip'
                    perfect for the moment

outside:
burnt capsicum on a barbecue
                    'a distinct dry hop character
                                        and crisp bitterness'

Blue Hills 107

from a concrete rotunda, Berry's Bay
moon and helicopter

the shoreline wooded, masts
from hidden boatyards

a crane swings on Milson's Point
as tiny dots climb the Bridge

Blue Hills 108

crow perches
on a wavering branch,
currawong edges up
an Illawarra flame,
the most fragile things
migrate: a mid-size orange,
a large black with white spots

I should walk somewhere
but why leave this soundscape

spend most of a day
doing ‘nothing in particular’

in my luggage
a rock paperweight
from another Botany Bay

Blue Hills 109

three-legged table
useless toaster
filing cabinet
barbecue labelled 'still works!'
numerous saucepans
one shoe (possibly added
        by a passer-by)

Blue Hills 110

the black beetle
disappears under
a fold of bark

*

what happens to
the scragged ends
of eucalypts?

*

branch die-off
sap drained
where no leaf grows

*

mosquito coil
near its end, the powder
arranged as a spiral below

*

on Unwin's Bridge
Road, the smell
of burnt biscuits

Homer Street

1

Turner would like it here
(the skies)

the city, northeast
as a ridge

separates creek
from river

a lone palm, almost
the tallest thing

2

water, fresh
and brackish
above and below
the dam

a rock
face, a
wall, of
what geology?

3

Sydney's microclimates:
the city obscured as a spot to the west lights up

a power outage on the northern beaches
ought to be visible

4

red and blue rectangles
the windows of the Catholic Church
the Anglican, diagonally back, sober brick

planes pass beyond the Greek delicatessen
the tails visible before they disappear behind
the Acropolis funeral parlour

5

the sky's romantic
but the architecture beneath is cubist;

the sensibility is surreal

at twilight the bats
fly to Five Dock

6

after a day of rain
the landscape returns:
Burwood, under construction,
Chatswood, is science fiction
orbited perhaps by tiny capsules,
then North Sydney, the city itself,
the white towers of Waterloo

7

clouds bank
at Rydalmere
all the way to Wiseman's Ferry
                                        later
                              shafts of light
hit the CBD

sharp outlines of buildings,
the distant hills

8

sunlight
                    opaque glass on the deck
lit up like a screen
waiting for shadows

this season swallows
dart in upper air
or skim the grasses of football ovals

9

a street of Californian bungalows,
red ochre and liver brick,
cream gables, timbered,
a black Norfolk pine

Canterbury race track under lights

the fireflies
                    (airliners)
approach Sydney
as they do
                morning and evening

hints of elsewhere
                        if we needed proof

10

cars cross the Wolli on Hartill-Law Avenue
Great Northern in the schooner
80s music on the Club's system
                (Love Resurrection)
the logo on the glass: HEADMASTER

there's no disposable plastic in here
(the world falls to bits outside)

water washes through sandstone
three ridges: Earlwood, Bardwell Park and Arncliffe
divide the Cooks River, Wolli and Bardwell Creeks
then the flat land towards Botany Bay

11

clouds, almost herringbone
suggest wind at altitude

an edge of sunlight
deepens in the room

12

rain blows in from southeast
misses this place

the skyline
blue over North Rocks

the northern beaches
obscure

as light breaks
on the deck

3 Afterimages

Michael Andrews

What if all the people you think you know
were just spots of light on canvas?

Arcimboldo

She's apples

Frank Auerbach

down Primrose Hill
two lights, feeble in middle ground,
hemmed in by shrubbery

orange visibility vests on a lime coloured oval
a street wet behind glass
pedestrians lit by the glow of phones

the open cigarette packet on the pub table
is a strategy, pencil backwards
on the interlocutor's ear

dusty window panes
haloed by sunlight
bright squares on a bar floor

Jacopo Bassano

Light breaks (or fades) over a distant mountain
but the figures in the foreground are too intent

to notice, animals marshalled up a ramp in pairs,
eggs collected in a basket. The humans

bundle possessions, sort copper pans, have
no time to view even the rising water.

To the left a monkey holds what looks like
a sceptre – has all sense deserted these people

alive in the cramped space of a jigsaw? All questions
seem to have an answer in this world

but where is the cat's companion?

François Boucher

only Cupid's chafed arse is real

Stella Bowen

a grand personage
unmoored in rubble
this is our history,

wallpaper exposed
as though the trees
of its pattern grew from

the stumps surrounding;
that aircrew, mapped
as though permanent

Alexander Calder

ballet shoes point upward
a slight figure, lifted

by a thickset one,
the weight of both

an absence, suggested
by continuous line

so the testes become a leg
an elbow becomes a signature

the space enclosed
animate;

across the aisle
Josephine Baker

dances, her shadow
lifeless on the wall

Caravaggio

the boy held down,
a hunk of meat,
not liking it

Grace Cossington Smith

it is best to knit things together
to see part of yourself
in the door of a mirrored robe
as a shadow against bright furniture

Gustave Courbet

The cliffs of Ornans appear
as they do through the gallery window,

the local characters enlarged, a bourgeois presumption
to be bigger than Napoleon (a short man),

to inhabit a large canvas, as though
worthy of the academy.

What made him present himself, greeted on the road
by another figure (engaged perhaps

in mere commerce) offer instead of an epithet
a commonplace?

William Dyce

It is October 5th 1858,
Donati's Comet visible

east off the Kent coast
at Pegwell Bay

(a precise date
and an angle)

'one of the most
beautiful objects

that I have ever seen',
bright for its century

and the fine weather,
bare smudges of cloud

the figures, observed
one evening months before,

collect shells and fossils,
oblivious to the future event

James Ensor

'embraced by a passionate squid'
at Ostend

(grey sea
forced such carnival, figuring

the end of a century
more than a calendar page;

exhumed from rubble,
the dead

tilt at each other;
as though someone

pulled a string and the puppets
lurched forward

to decorate the mayoral suite
with their entrails

Ian Fairweather

a wall haunted by depth
crowded, flat as Javanese cloth:
what recedes and what advances
in this jungle?

Jean-Honoré Fragonard

the swing, a device
to expose underclothing, or

a tragedy of uncertain times:
the hunt for a slipper in the bushes?

Ian Friend

figure and ground shift
as ovals and dots lose focus

forms dissolve when damp,
grow clear and sharp when dry,

with half-closed eyes shapes move
impossible to shift by impulse,

bones calcify and shrink,
parts of what we are

gather and disperse
in a humid atmosphere;

what surrounds
is one substance

Angela Gardner

human bones etched
as x-ray
are a forest

a ravine might consist
of a gap between
cut-up papers

to edit
or accumulate
a question

are these marks
sufficient
on this surface

a palimpsest
transparent or
opaque, nothing

more than this,
or less

Alberto Giacometti

i'm
a mere

mortal
a

tool
a bottle

i'm
a limb

a
game

a mir-
age

i'm
gloom

Mona Hatoum

Domesticities (bedframes, toys)
wired up and lethal,

nothing's for certain:
a cheese-grater divides a room;

light through
a wire cage casts

shadows, induces vertigo;
a propeller,

one blade furrowed,
the other straight,

makes a pattern
in sand, then erases it

Barbara Hepworth

am I
highly strung,

or am I
a chiseller figuring

the relative density
of stone and wood

David Jones

all things inscribed:
the great tree
seen through glass
a conduit
from Brockley
to paradise

Basil King

The face could be
lunar, its craters

the glint of an eye,
bend sinister of the mouth;

half is in eclipse,
an orange shadow,

the other half glances out
at invisible events,

history maybe, or
just a present

occurring somewhere
behind you;

a glow, or
halo surrounds it

Paul Klee

is the key

Peter Lanyon

those quadrilaterals,
hedges, a landing strip
seen through cross-hairs

that line, a strut or cliff edge
a sudden dip or buffet
a broad slash of blue

landscape, suggested once by a Claude glass
might be just this . . . this . . . this,
like ornithology: 'for the birds'

Christiane Löhr

hair

line

Godfrey Miller

would it be possible
to mathematise experience of shape,
the fruit, the jug,
their anatomy?

you could read that pattern of light
as a series of diamonds, a belief
in the diagonal

would this be theology?

Dorothy Napangardi

It's the double negative,
the not not there that holds you:
tracks where there seem to be none,
contours of sand, salt lines
converging in a dip.

Wavering colours behind the nets
regroup when you alter focus.
Does the dark recede or advance?

A square of linen may measure space
when the space we know is destroyed.
On a white wall, somewhere else maps itself out
and the daylight streets are not the same.

Paul Nash

As if those clumps (Wittenham)
stood against the sky
in supplication

or if this bollard were a visitor
from across the Channel
lost on a grey beach

or this fragmented wood,
that mud hole, a place in which
some strange object might grow

Sidney Nolan

colour has no decorum:
an Eastern Rosella
perches where it can

a flat landscape
brushed with ripolin
imitates suburbia

from the hilltop dunny
you can see for miles

they call it civilisation
over here

Georgia O'Keeffe

under blue sky
a dark door
in a wall of mud

Eduardo Paolozzi

when *Popular Mechanics* meets *Intimate Confessions*
the human body becomes an assemblage:

kiss me quick, squeeze me slow
translates as the bright, clean future

Pablo Picasso

'no arse holes
in my gallery'
just a curve, repeated

things seem without purpose,
this constant drawing, erasure, drawing again,
suddenly it comes together

in the middle room of the exhibition,
nudes with mirrors
a slash of vermillion leaps out

Nicolas Poussin

Masks, panpipes, heads of artichokes,
the face of Pan, beetroot red

(elsewhere, armless and legless
though the testes and penis remain intact).

Statuary in unearthly light
glows from the shrubbery,

dancers' feet rhyme
with the hooves of beasts.

The tone, the placement
of these elements is perfect

to what effect (if not belief):
the wry expression of the painter?

Robert Rauschenberg

bombs fall on whatever flux
(are those bedsheets mine)?

what does the *Saturday Evening Post*
have to say about *this*:

a stuffed goat
on tenterhooks?

this politic is a body that
plants a flag on a lunar surface,

whose ads are texts for
the new opera;

erasure makes memory
greater than the thing itself

Auguste Rodin

when you touch the back of the head
with your heel

your body becomes
a letter of the alphabet,

your sex
never so apparent;

ink wash leaves
room to manoeuvre

when hands play
with substance;

arcs of musculature
reversed in plaster

come alive as bronze

Ken Searle

a pick, an ancient projector,
a potato masher, an aeroplane in flight
over an ashtray, an empty beer bottle
green stalk protruding, a lily, prone
on a table with peeling paint

memento mori in
South Australian sunlight

through the louvres, a possible clothesline,
the roof of a carport

Georges Seurat

motion is predicated
on the interaction of colour

our relation with others
apart at intervals

an equation,
a chemical reaction

the way gaslight makes
shape uncertain

and objects stutter
in its aura

Martin Sharp

In response to a photograph
(my father, dressed for Shakespeare

before a hillside of dead eucalypts
circa 1920)

a painted playing card,
a little royal, a little Chinese,

two figures in strange hats, posed
as a theatre bill:

an item, rescued
from a burnt-out amusement park

by an archaeologist
of remembered pleasure

Gherardo Starnina

The huts are too dispersed
for a village,

the crags about them
an unlikely geography

where boats on a river
dwarfed by figures on the far shore

ply their trade as if
the habitations were cities.

An angel rockets from a dark sky
into this world of commerce

governed by hermits on crutches.
On the horizon a bearded man

menaced by a small bear
clings to a bush

David Strachan

At the Ervin Gallery utensils hang
intense as the teeth of Tucker's demons;

across Kent St a man places a saucepan on a gas range
out on the balcony of a terrace.

Tintoretto

I believe this:
that the putti are planets

that all things
hang from a centre

that I live in a city where
perspective turns on itself

Tony Tuckson

all elbows
like a jazz band

those L's took off
all by themselves

a rhyming slang
of right angles

held together
on yellow newsprint

Maria Helena Vieria da Silva

the city
in slivers:

transparent
as the body politic is opaque

Brett Whiteley

be like a god
drunk on literature

wear a white robe
make an entrance

paint from your tower
the blue harbour

reminder of our tourist selves
know this and more

tear a canvas
install a light behind it

the source of everything
a hole in the arm

John Wolseley

trace on a map
a journey:

as an insect
burrows through wood

beneath rubbings and
leaf-mould

shards and veins
as negatives

A note on the poems

The poems in this book include some written during my last year in Britain (based mostly in Faversham, a market town in east Kent) and others written on a visit to Australia in 2016 and after my return in October 2018. 'Allotments' continue a loose series, the first 100 of which appear in the book of the same name, published by Shearsman (Bristol, 2014) while the 'Blue Hills' poems continue from much earlier work done in Australia between 1980 and 2006, numbering 1 to 75 and spread out over several volumes reassembled by Puncher & Wattman as *The Collected Blue Hills* (Sydney, 2012). There's no need to go back to the earlier work in order to understand what's going on in either case though you might well want to do so. The poems in the final section, 'Afterimages', are not strictly ekphrastic works. Some do 'describe' paintings, some are comments on artists and some are imaginary constructions of what a particular artist *might* have done. The intention all along was to make poems that worked as poems without depending upon the 'original' art.

The Giramondo Publishing Company acknowledges the support of Western Sydney University in the implementation of its book publishing program.

This project has been assisted by the Commonwealth Government through the Australia Council, its arts funding and advisory body.